ALL YEAR R

Spring

Kathleen Edwardes

Based on the Central television programmes

Macdonald Educational

HOW TO USE THIS BOOK

First, look at the contents page opposite. The chapter list tells you what each page is about.

If you want to know about one particular thing, look it up in the index on page 30. For example, if you want to know about skin, the index tells you that there is something about it on pages 8, 24 and 25. The index also lists the pictures in the book.

When you read this book, you will find some unusual words. The glossary on pages 28–29 explains what they mean.

Editor
Claire Llewellyn

Design
Liz Black

Production
Marguerite Fenn

Picture research
Diana Morris

Factual adviser
M G Ayres

Teacher panel
Mary Gribbin
Frances Scott

The poem on page 11 is included with the kind permission of Hodder & Stoughton.

Illustrations
Lynn Breeze: 20, 21
Peter Bull: 18 (top)
John Farman: 12, 22–3, 25
Toni Goffe: 11, 18–19
Robert Morton: 9
Cynthia Pow: 7, 24
Kate Rogers: 15, 26, 27
Larry Ronstadt: front cover
Sylvia Tate: 6, 13, 17

Photographs
Barnaby's Picture Library: 26 (right)
Bruce Coleman/Jane Burton: 16
Sally & Richard Greenhill: 10
Camilla Jessel: 6, 8, 26 (centre right)
NHPA/Stephen Dalton: 14
Science Photo Library: 24
Zefa: 14 (right), 26 (left and centre left)

CONTENTS

GROWING

Growing and changing

Who is the oldest person you know? – Perhaps a grandparent or neighbour. Look at some old photos together. Try to recognize the person you know. Do they look like that now? Think about how you've changed, and how you might change in the future.

All through life you grow and change in many ways.

	Me as a baby	Me now	Me as a teenager
toys	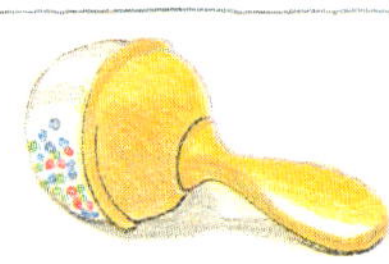		
shoes			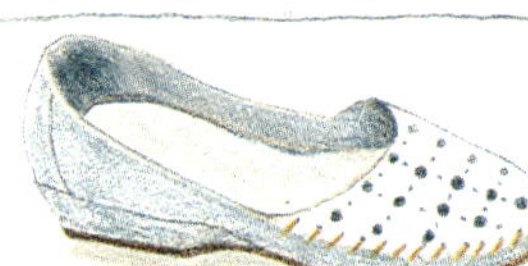
food			

Make a growing and changing chart for yourself. Will it look like this? What is missing on this chart?

It's fun to watch things grow and change. Peas, beans, potatoes and the seeds of some flowers are all easy to grow, and you can keep a close watch on what happens. All living things grow, live their life and die. All the time they slowly change. To help you grow, you need air, food and drink, exercise and rest, shelter and warmth, love and care. Do your seeds need the same things as you?

You could grow a pea or bean using blotting paper and sawdust in a jam jar.

A potato will grow in water in a narrow-necked jar.

Grow nasturtium seeds in a tray of potting compost.

GROWING

Year by year

All your friends in your class at school are about the same age. You probably know who is the youngest and oldest. If not, it's easy to find out. But how can you tell how old people are if you can't ask them? There are clues to help you. Look at their skin. Is it wrinkled? Look at the colour of their hair. But – be careful! – is it only old people that have grey hair? Listen to their voice. Look at their teeth and their hands. Compare them with your own. Watch how they move. Now guess how old some of your friends and relations are. How close were you?

Arrange the children from the youngest to the oldest. What clues will help you?

You can find out the age of other things too – a tree, for example, and its twigs.

Examine a twig on the branch of a tree. You will see different marks on it. Some are leaf scars, where leaves once grew. Some are ring scars. They go right round a twig and mark the place where a terminal bud once grew. Count the ring scars to find the twig's age.

Looking ahead

Growing up is a little like going on a journey. You pass many interesting and different sights on the way. Some things you may always remember, like losing your first tooth or having a special birthday treat.

Do you ever wonder what might happen when you're older? It's not just your body that grows. Your mind grows too. You talk, listen and read. You learn many things about the world.

Big bricks are easy to hold. Young children use them to make simple models.

When you grow older, you can build complex models. Your interests change too.

You can't depend on anything

When I was just a little boy
I used to race about
and kick the empty rubbish tins
that people had left out.
I'm older
and know better now,
we learn things as we grow,
the tin that I just kicked was full
and nearly broke my toe.

Peggy Dunstan

Wash and brush up

It's fun to have a shower or bath, to feel fresh and look clean. Washing is only one part of looking after yourself. How do you care for your hands, nails, hair, teeth, feet, shoes, clothes and all the other things that belong to you? Does anyone help you?

Some jobs need doing every day, some once a week. Which jobs need doing less often? There are times when you take extra special care with how you look. There are other times when you have to get dirty. When are they? Some people seem to enjoy getting dirty. Do you?

Imagine what it would be like if you never washed.

Animals need to be clean too. Some like water. Others keep clean without water. Some roll on the ground. Some lick themselves and clean each other. Others need our help. These are the animals we keep as our pets.

Animal homes have to be kept clean too. In the wild, birds drop their waste out of the nest. The rabbit kicks its waste out of the burrow. Pet birds, rabbits and hamsters need your help. Their cage and bedding, food and water containers all need regular cleaning. How often would you clean out a pet's cage?

Each of these animals keeps clean in a different way. Do you know how?

KEEPING CLEAN

Cleaning up the world

This dead bee is food for ants. They are carrying it back to their nest.

Seagulls feed on waste tips where they scavenge for scraps of food.

People are not good at keeping places clean. Our litter clutters up the countryside and towns. Can you think why litter is such a bad thing? What would happen if it was never collected? Birds, animals and insects are good cleaners. They are not tidying up for us. They are feeding and keeping themselves alive, but they do leave everywhere cleaner.

Even in spring, you can still find leaves which fell from the trees in autumn. Some will have started to rot. If you go for a walk you might see other things that are rotting. Does everything rot? Be a scientist and try to find out.

This rotting leaf will mix with the soil to make food for other plants.

Collect some fallen leaves, some soil, and some ring pulls from old cans. Put them all in a polythene bag. Water the soil. Fasten the bag with a twist. Keep it in a warm dark place for about eight weeks. Can you guess what you might find?

What other things could you use instead of ring pulls? What could you use instead of leaves?

KEEPING SAFE

Sense that danger

Look at the rabbit in the picture. See how alert it is. It's standing up on its back legs to have a good look all round. Its ears are pricked up to hear every sound. Its nose is twitching. What can it smell? The rabbit senses danger and will dart to the safety of its burrow.

Animals listen, watch and smell all the time. They use their senses to keep safe and to stay alive.

Think of the senses this rabbit is using. You too must sense the dangers around you.

Can you sense danger? Look outside. What can you see? Now listen carefully. What can you hear? Use your senses to spot dangers at home, too. Go into your kitchen. Have a good look round. How do you know what is hot or sharp? What is safe to touch? Is anything safe to taste? Your five senses – smelling, hearing, seeing, touching and tasting – warn you wherever you are, at home, at school, when you're going to the shops or looking for a place to play. Take notice of what they tell you and learn to sense danger. In the end it's up to you.

Your senses can save you from being hurt. Which of them would warn you of these dangers?

KEEPING SAFE

Is anywhere safe?

There are many signs that warn us of danger. Make a list of the ones near your school or home. Do you know what they all mean?

You could draw some signs of your own. What would you put in a sign to warn people about dangers like building sites, railway lines or a frozen pond?

These signs warn us of certain dangers. Do you know what they mean?

Keep Out! Caution! No Entry! are warnings. They tell you that a place isn't safe. But not all unsafe places have warnings like these, and nowhere can be safe all the time. When you want to play, you must find the right place for your game. Where would you go to play hide-and-seek, sail a toy boat, fly a kite or run with a dog? The best place is the safest place and it's up to you to find it.

People can be hazards too. Look very carefully at this busy street. How many dangers can you spot? Danger-spotting may prevent accidents.

KEEPING SAFE

Safe risk-taking

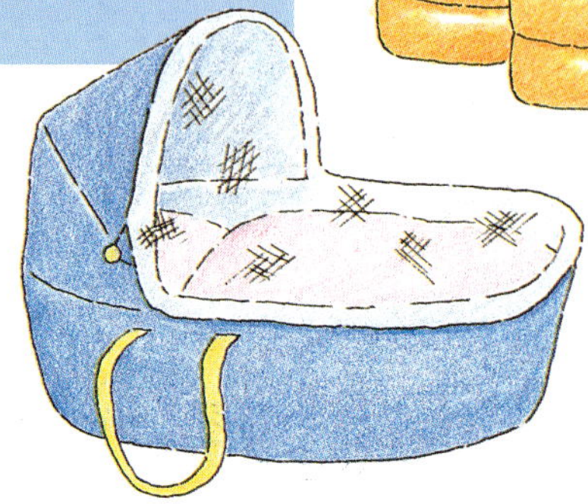

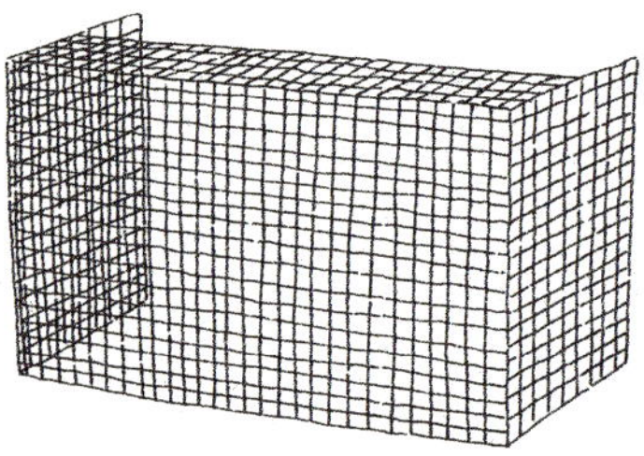

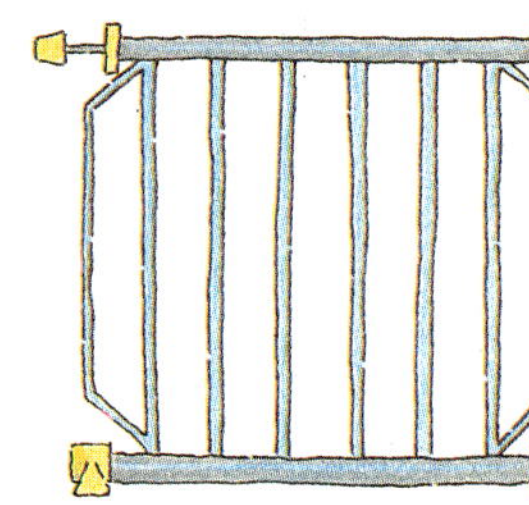

How do these things keep a baby safe?

As you grow older, you learn to take care of yourself. But you may still need adults to help you in traffic or near water. Adults must 'think safe' too. They can't do without help either.

What's missing from each of these pictures?
Can you make these people safe?

Life can seem full of dangers sometimes. We need to understand the dangers and keep ourselves as safe as we can. We need to be safe risk-takers. What safety rules do you have at school? Do you think they are good ones? As you grow older, you have to decide how best to keep safe. Start now. Think about riding a bike. Find a safe place to practise. Get some training from an adult. Be sure you can ride your bike safely before you go on the roads.

Look at this boy's bike. What needs doing before it's safe to ride? Make sure your bike is safe too.

In good working order

Just think how busy you are all day long. It's a full-time job keeping yourself in good working order. Think about the start you make to each day to prepare for all you are going to do. You will need lots of energy. Eating breakfast helps. What you eat, and when you eat it, is important. Do you know why?

Lots of love and care and a sound night's sleep will put you back in good working order after all the day's thinking, working, eating and playing.

Your body needs exercise every day. The food you eat gives it the energy to do all the things you want to do. But it can't go on non-stop. Sometimes it needs to rest. How do you know when you need a rest? What do you like to do when you rest? Something quietly by yourself, perhaps, or with someone you love.

In need of repair

However well you look after yourself, you can't always be fit and healthy. Sometimes you are in need of repair – often when you've bumped your skin. Skin covers you all over. It protects you from germs, especially if you keep its tiny pores clean and fresh.

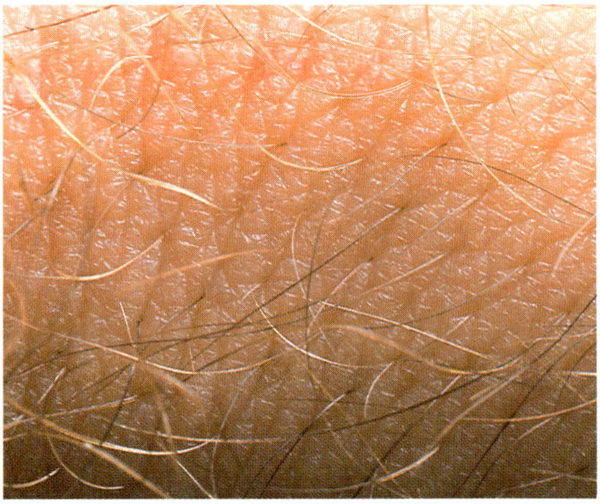

Look at your skin through a hand lens. What can you see?

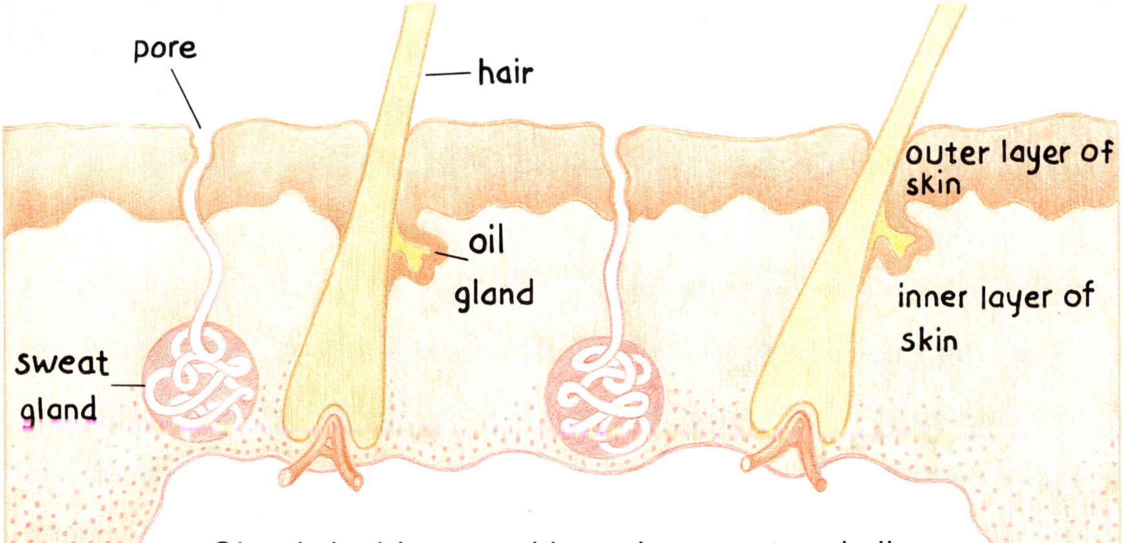

Glands inside your skin make sweat and oil. Sweat keeps the skin cool. What does oil do?

Have you ever seen a dog lick a cut paw until it heals? When you cut your finger, you too need to keep it clean. This may stop germs getting inside your body. If harmful germs do enter the cut, your body needs to be able to fight them off. This happens in the blood, where there are special substances called white blood cells that destroy germs. The body also makes antibodies. These make germs harmless. Can you think of any other ways you can hurt your skin besides cutting it?

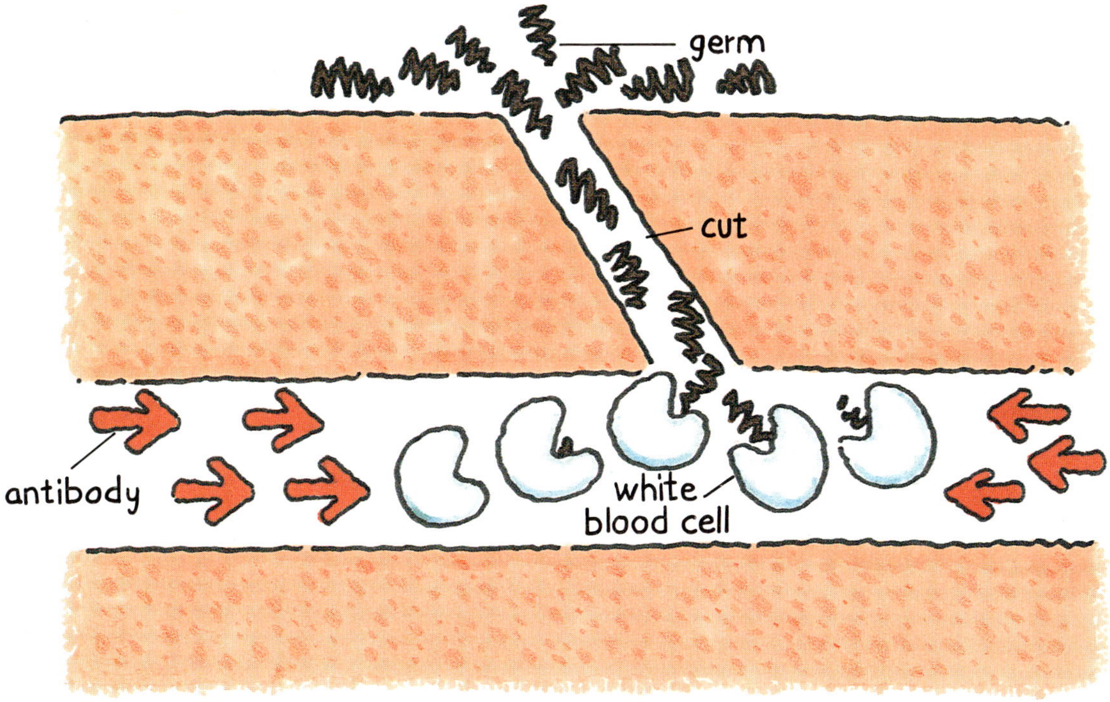

In the blood, white cells surround and destroy harmful germs. Antibodies also join in the attack.

KEEPING HEALTHY

Feeling good all over

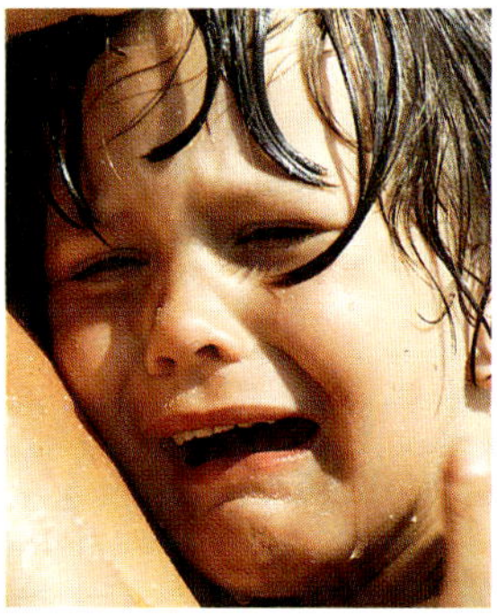

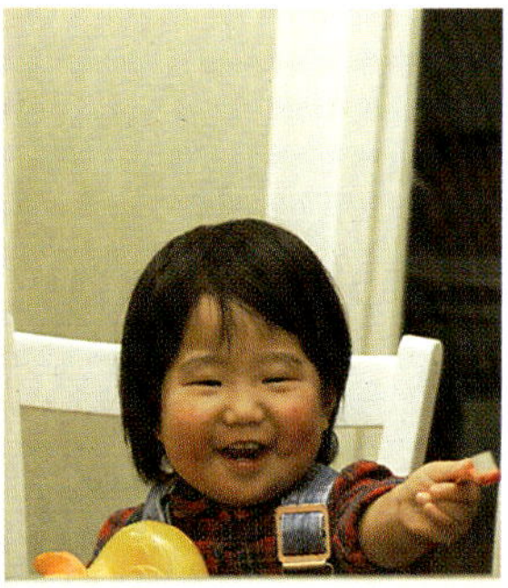

Look at these children. Can you guess what they are thinking or how they are feeling?

Look in the mirror. What can you see? Are you feeling sad, frightened, excited, proud, silly, embarrassed, happy? How you feel can show on your face and also in how you behave. Try acting out some feelings for your friends to guess. Sometimes you want to share how you feel with others. Sometimes you keep it to yourself.

You share your feelings with someone you trust. Who do you go to?

Your brain controls everything you do and feel. You use it to think, to make up your mind, to work out problems. It makes you different from anyone else. That makes you special.

Feeling good is a part of being healthy. Think of all the things that make you feel good, then draw them on jigsaw pieces and make your own 'Feeling Good All Over' jigsaw. It might include someone you love, something you're good at, or something you treasure. Joined together, the pieces make you a complete, happy and healthy person. Try and stay that way. It's up to you!

What would you add if this was your jigsaw?

GLOSSARY

cell	A tiny part of your body. Your whole body is made of many millions of tiny cells.
compare	You compare two things when you look closely at them to see how they are different and how they are the same.
complex	If a model is complex, it has lots of parts and can be difficult to put together.
germ	A tiny living thing which lives in the body, on food or on dirt. It can make you ill.
gland	Part of the body that makes a special substance to help the body to work well. There are many kinds of glands.
oil	A fatty liquid that helps to stop things getting too dry.

pore	A tiny hole that allows sweat to come out onto the skin.
scavenge	A bird scavenges when it feeds from rotting rubbish.
scientist	A person who makes careful studies and tests.
sense	When you sense danger, you feel it without knowing why.
sweat	A liquid which comes out from the body through the pores in the skin. It cools you when you work hard or when it is hot.
terminal bud	The terminal bud is the bud at the end of a stem.
waste	Food which is not useful to your body and which leaves it when you go to the toilet.

INDEX

The **dark** numbers show you where there is a picture of the subject.